AMALIENBORG AND FREDERIKSSTADEN

The Palace and the Royal Quarter

by Jens Gunni Busck

Historika

Published in cooperation with the Royal Danish Collection

Frederiksstaden comprises, strictly speaking, the buildings between Bredgade and Toldbodgade, and it stretches from St Annæ Plads to the street now called Esplanaden. Here an early phase of the development of the district is seen in a section of Christian Geddes's map from 1757. At that stage the Amalienborg palaces and the other great mansions of the district had been completed, and so had a large number of the bourgeois houses, as well as Frederik's Hospital (the square building which is now Designmuseum Danmark). On the map one can also see where Frederik's Church was planned, on the other side of Bredgade, although construction work there had hardly begun when the map was drawn.

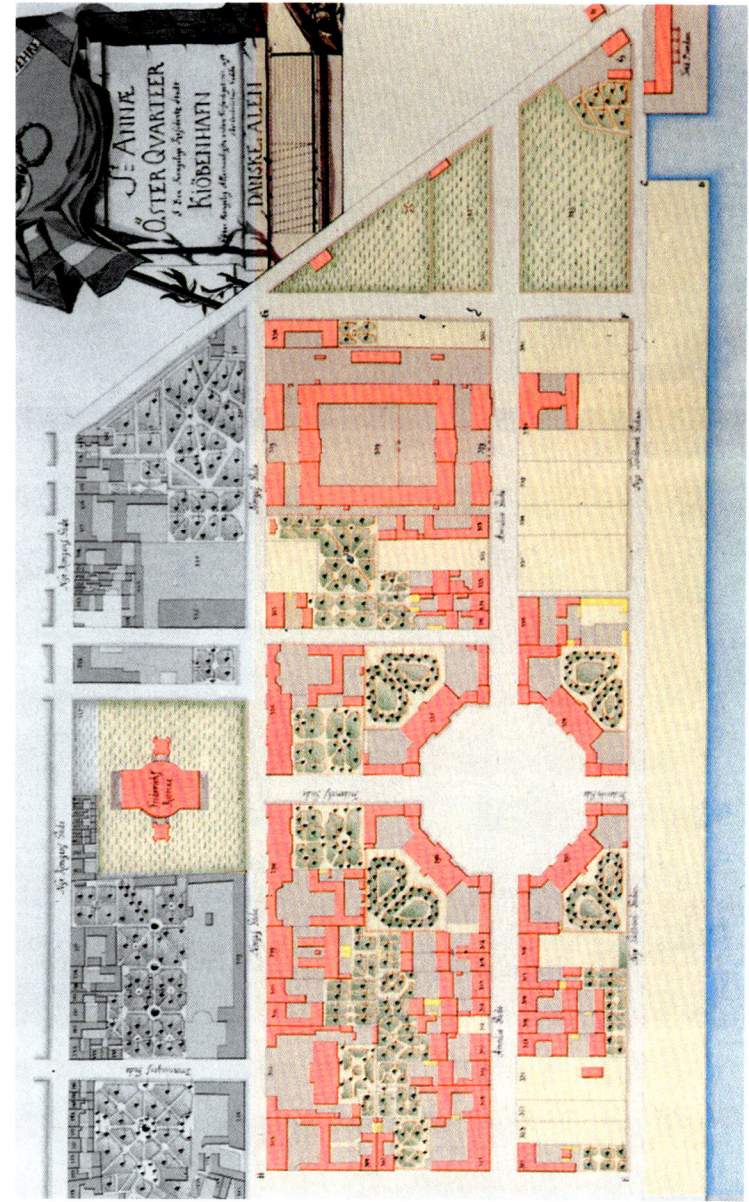

CONTENTS

Preface   5

"Spot the difference" – palaces   7
   The Royal Standards   12

Amalienborg and Frederiksstaden   14
   Earlier history   17
   The founding of Frederiksstaden   21
   The main features of the town plan   23
   Building Frederiksstaden   29
      Amalienborg   30
      The equestrian statue   31
      Frederik's Church (the Marble Church)   37
   Royalty at Amalienborg   38
      Christian VII (1766-1808)   38
      Frederik VI (1808-1839)   42
      Christian VIII (1839-1848)   42
      Frederik VII (1848-1863)   45
      Christian IX (1863-1906)   45
      Frederik VIII (1906-1912)   46
      Christian X (1912-1947)   46
      Frederik IX (1947-1972)   50
   Amalienborg today   53

Bibliography and further reading   58

Visit Amalienborg   59

FOREWORD

Amalienborg has been the capital city residence of the Danish Royal House for more than 200 years and is visited by thousands of guests from Denmark and other countries every year. The four palaces and the equestrian statue in the middle of the square constitute the centre of Frederiksstaden, the surrounding quarter of Copenhagen.

This little book tells the story of Amalienborg and Frederiksstaden and also answers the question most frequently asked by visitors: Where does the Queen live?

Birgit Jenvold
Museum Curator

Amalienborg and the Frederiksstaden axis, west at the top.

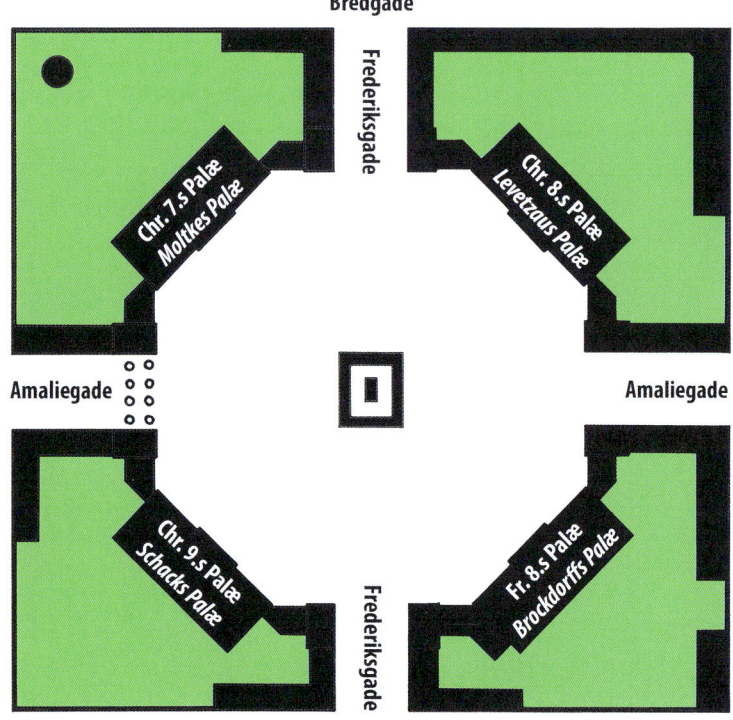

6 Amalienborg and Frederiksstaden

"SPOT THE DIFFERENCE" – PALACES

The four palaces that make up Amalienborg are very familiar to most Danes and to many foreigners. Both the "birds'eye" view of the palaces and their facades are imprinted on the memory if one has been to the open square between them and/or seen the royal residence on television, on the Internet, or in magazines or books.

But how can you tell the difference between the four palaces? There are actually a few quite simple distinguishing features, and the following pages will explain them, as well as illustrating the royal flags.

Christian IX's Palace. Seen from the harbour side the palace is in the foreground on the left. It is the only one of the Amalienborg Palaces that has five chimneys. The palace is the residence of Her Majesty the Queen and His Royal Highness the Prince Consort.
(Previous name: Schack's Palace.)

Frederik VIII's Palace. Seen from the harbour side the palace is in the foreground on the right. It is the only one of the Amalienborg Palaces that has a clock in the facade on the square. The Palace is the residence of their Royal Highnesses Crown Prince Frederik and Crown Princess Mary. (Previous name: Brockdorff's Palace.)

"Spot the difference" – palaces

Christian VII's Palace. Seen from the harbour side the palace is furthest to the left and has three chimneys. The central door onto the square is yellowish brown, while the doors of the other three palaces are dark green. The building is used for representative purposes, e.g. for banquets and as a guest residence for State Visits. (Previous name: Moltke's Palace.)

"Spot the difference" – palaces

Christian VIII's Palace. Seen from the harbour side the palace is furthest to the right. The building has four chimneys, and there is no clock on the facade. This building houses the Amalienborg Museum, Her Majesty the Queen's Reference Library and accommodation for Their Royal Highnesses Prince Joachim and Princess Marie and for Her Royal Highness Princess Benedikte. (Previous name: Levetzau's Palace.)

The Royal Standards

The Royal Standards are used by the Royal House, e.g. to mark the presence of a member of the Royal Family. The standards consist of Dannebrog as a swallow-tailed flag with a central field on which there is a special emblem.

The swallow-tailed flag is in general used only by the Royal House and the State. Swallow-tailed flags are flown at Amalienborg on official flag days if members of the Royal Family are not in residence in the palaces.

12   Amalienborg and Frederiksstaden

The Monarch's Standard is Her Majesty the Queen's flag with the large national coat of arms, known as the Royal Crest, in the central field.

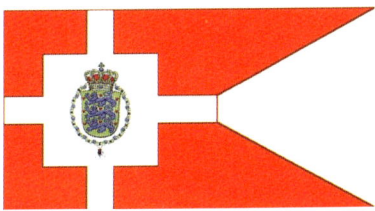

The Standard of the Heir to the Throne, His Royal Highness the Crown Prince, has the lesser national coat of arms, known as the state coat of arms, in the central field, surrounded by the chain of the Order of the Elephant.

The Standard of His Royal Highness the Prince Consort has the Prince Consort's crest in the central field.

The Regent's Standard carries the Royal Regalia in the central field: the Crown, the Sceptre, the Sword of State and the Orb. This standard is flown for His Royal Highness Prince Joachim or Her Royal Highness Princess Benedikte when either of them is functioning as Regent.

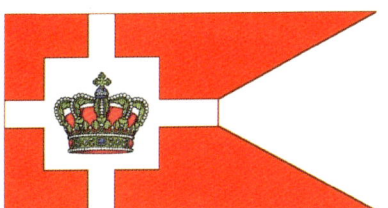

The Royal Standard has the Royal Crown in the central field and is used for other members of the Royal Family.

The Royal Standards

AMALIENBORG AND FREDERIKSSTADEN

The district of Frederiksstaden in Copenhagen was built in the 1750s and stretches from Sankt Annæ Plads (Saint Anne's Square) to the street called Esplanaden, between Toldbodgade and Bredgade. This little segment of town is part of the larger Sankt Annæ Øster Kvarter (Eastern Saint Anne's Quarter), which is the old name for the area framed by Nyhavn, Store Kongensgade and Kastellet (the Citadel). Frederiksstaden is cut across by two streets that form axes – Amaliegade and Frederiksgade, and at their intersection in Amalienborg Palace Square there is the magnificent equestrian statue of Frederik V, in whose honour this district of the town was built. The king sits high up on horseback, facing the church which bears his name, Frederiks Kirke, and he is surrounded by four elegant palaces in rococo style; the ensemble is considered to be one of Europe's best-composed building-works from the 18th century.

If one stands on Amalienborg Palace Square and takes in the particularly harmonious refinement that characterizes its octagonal structure, it is difficult to imagine that the triumphant horseman in the centre was in reality an alcoholic who was deeply unhappy with his royal role. Frederik V's great deficiencies in the role of God's representative did not in any way diminish the limitlessly lavish royal glorification that was prevalent in the heyday of the absolute monarchy, and which saw its culmination in Frederiksstaden. The construction of this area of the town took place in the context of a period of economic prosperity in which ministers of state, noblemen, merchants and talented craftsmen were all willing to make efforts for the cause of enhancing royal prestige, and even in its actual physical composition Frederiksstaden was a form of homage to royal power.

It is nonetheless the case that Amalienborg was not at all originally intended as a royal residence. The primary royal residence at the time was the newly-built Christiansborg Palace, which provided an extremely imposing and stately milieu, and Frederik V would hardly in his wildest dreams have imagined living in the new area of town that had been

Frederik V, painted by Carl Gustav Pilo. Supposedly, the portrait shows the king immediately after his anointment on 4 September 1747; several copies painted during the subsequent years exist. Despite his popularity with the people, Frederik V was entirely unsuited for kingship, and he left the governing of the kingdom to more competent politicians – particularly Lord Chamberlain A.G. Moltke, who was the central driving force behind the construction of Frederiksstaden.

built in his honour. It was therefore quite by accident that Amalienborg's four palaces, which were originally built as private mansions for noblemen, came to function so well as residences for the Royal Family. When Christiansborg was destroyed by fire in 1794 there was an urgent need for an alternative residence, and that was the reason that Amalienborg became the Royal Family's permanent address in Copenhagen.

Amalienborg is thus not just a typical royal palace – it is in the strictest sense not actually a palace. The palace square was renamed "Amalienborg Slotsplads" (Amalienborg Palace Square) a few years ago, but previously it was known as "Amalienborg Plads" and earlier still it was called "Frederiks Plads". It is a mistake, although a common one, to speak of "Amalienborg Slot"; in Danish the correct name is simply "Amalienborg" or "the Amalienborg Palaces", reflecting the origins of the buildings as mansions for the nobility. This is also demonstrated in the peculiar fact that each of the palaces has two names – an earlier one relating to its original noble owner and a newer official name stemming from one of the kings that later lived in it.

The Amalienborg axis seen from the top of the dome of Frederik's Church.

Earlier history

Until the 17th century Copenhagen was still contained within its old medieval ramparts, which on the north-east side ran across what is now Kongens Nytorv. In 1606 Christian IV began to buy up an extensive area outside the medieval town, and in the course of the 1630s and 40s he had large ramparts and moats built around this area; considerable sections of these are preserved now in the Botanical Gardens and the park area called Østre Anlæg. The area of the town was doubled by this process, and inside the new ramparts Christian IV succeeded in building himself a residence – Rosenborg Castle with the surrounding gardens, Kongens Have – and the naval housing area of Nyboder, as well as constructing the beginnings of a never-completed round church.

There was plenty of space left, however, and Frederik III's Queen, Sophie Amalie, used some of it in the 1660s to launch the building of a "pleasure palace" approximately on the site where present-day Amalienborg stands. The palace was meant to serve as a replacement for "the Queen's Enghave" (the Queen's garden), a Renaissance garden near where Tivoli is now located which was destroyed during the Swedish siege of Copenhagen in 1658-59. The project required the filling in of the marshy areas between the shore and Norgesgade (present-day Bredgade), which was the main traffic artery of the new area of town. By order of the King all of the town's waste was taken out there

Sophie Amalienborg, which burned down in 1689. Painted by J.J. Bruun in 1740 on the basis of earlier paintings. Rosenborg Castle.

so that it became possible to build on the ground, and the result was Denmark's first baroque palace, Sophie Amalienborg, which was completed in 1673. It was an imposing Italian-inspired villa, which stood approximately at the end of the present Fredericiagade and had a splendid, extravagant interior – including a kind of primitive lift.

The palace lent emphasis to the refined character of the new quarter of town, and in the following years it provided the venue for a number of magnificent court occasions. These continued after the death of Queen Sophie Amalie in 1685, but came to an abrupt end in 1689, when Christian V's 44th birthday was being celebrated. A proper party for the absolute monarch necessarily involved an opera, and a temporary playhouse of pinewood had been set up for this purpose, close to the palace. The birthday performance for the town's elite was a great success, and in the following days repeat performances were staged for a younger audience from the aristocracy and the upper bourgeoisie. The narrative involved the Roman gods and fireworks with smoke effects, but during the third performance some of the decorations caught fire, causing the playhouse to burn down within fifteen minutes. The doors could only be opened inwards, and because of the ensuing panic only a few people escaped with their lives. About 180 people, most of them children, lost their lives, and the fire spread further to the palace, which burned to the ground within a few hours.

The fire that destroyed Sophie Amalienborg was for decades considered to be the great catastrophe of the time, and it was the subject of innumerable melancholy memorial poems and songs. One can still today find reminders of the tragedy in several places in Copenhagen – for instance, a student residence, Elers' Kollegium, was erected in memory of its founder's children, who died in the fire. The name Amalienborg continued to be associated with the site and was thus inherited by the new buildings that were embarked on there sixty years later.

In the course of the 1690s Christian V considered several plans for a new residential palace on the site of Sophie Amalienborg, including a proposal drawn up by the Swedish court architect Nicodemus Tessin, but nothing was put in hand before Christian V's death in 1699, and when the Great Nordic War broke out in 1700 the idea of Swedish cooperation had to be ruled out. The site was therefore left undeveloped until the 1720s, when a royal pleasure garden was laid out in the area closest to the town, with a parade ground in proximity to Kastellet, the Citadel. Between those two areas an octagonal pavilion was erected; its form can be said to have anticipated that of Amalienborg. In the intervening years Frederik IV had made his own contribution to royal building projects

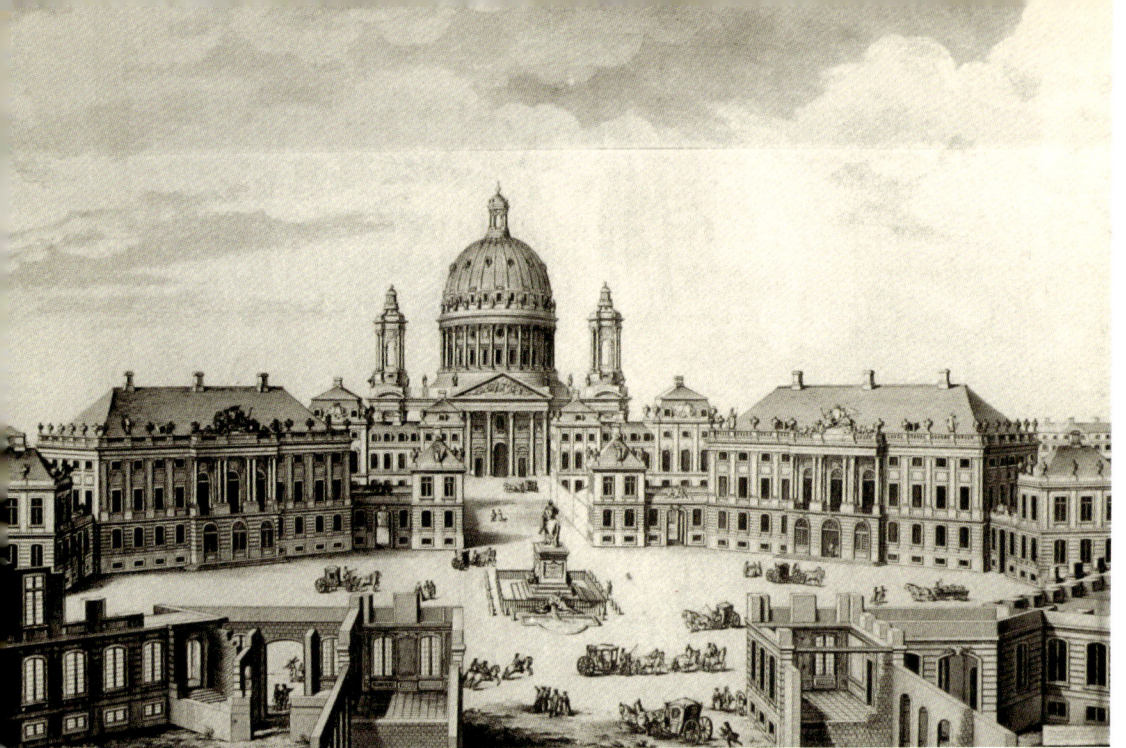

Idealized view of Amalienborg, 1766. Engraving by J.M. Preisler from a drawing by L.A. le Clerc. From Den Danske Vitruvius III.

by initiating Fredensborg Palace, north of Copenhagen, and Frederiksberg Palace, in the western part of the town. In the 1730s, when Christian VI had the first Christiansborg Palace built in the centre of Copenhagen, there was no longer any thought of building a palace on the Amalienborg site. The palace of Christiansborg, which was completed in 1740, was perhaps the most splendid royal palace in Northern Europe and was the pride of the kingdom for the half century of its existence before it burned down in 1794.

The founding of Frederiksstaden

A few years after Frederik V's accession to the throne, in August 1749, the empty Amalienborg site became the focus of attention once again when a group of powerful merchants put forward a proposal for development of the area, in which they at that time had timber yards on the shore. The proposal was rapidly reconceived at a higher level, primarily thanks to the influence of Lord Chamberlain A.G. Moltke, who was a kind of father-figure for Frederik V. Because of the King's dissolute lifestyle Moltke functioned as unofficial prime minister and was in fact the most powerful man in the country. He saw the possibility to use the building project to pay homage to the King and the absolute

Memorial plaque to Nicolai Eigtved on the wall of the side building to Christian VIII's Palace in Frederiksgade.

monarchy. This was actually already in process, in that the 300th anniversary of the ruling Oldenburg Royal House (which strictly speaking happened in the previous year) was to be celebrated with large-scale festivities on 28-30 October 1749.

The opportunity thus presented itself to construct a new district of town as an appropriate way of honouring the King at this juncture, and a group of citizens who were eager to develop the town in this way were ready to act to realize the project. A plan was worked out to expedite the construction work and at the same time allow Frederik V to appear in an extremely generous light: the King could transfer the area to the Copenhagen town authority, which could administer the allocation of sites and organize the construction work. Citizens would receive free sites on which to build, together with easing of customs and taxes due, so long as they constructed a new building within five years and respected rules for building which would ensure a high degree of uniformity. By 12 September Frederik V was able to announce the plan to construct Frederiksstaden on the basis of this scheme, and work went ahead immediately to allocate sites to prosperous members of the nobility and the higher bourgeoisie – people who would be able to meet the heavy demands, in terms of building requirements, attached to the royal donation. The allocations were of course made in such a way that the finest of the new owners received the most attractive sites, i.e. the sites on Bredgade and those around the central square.

The new area of town was intended to be characterized by the greatest possible "equality and regularity" and thus make amends for a significant deficiency in the Danish capital. The sweeping lines of baroque were known from elsewhere, including Stockholm, St Petersburg and especially Paris, but in the middle of the century Copenhagen still looked like a medieval town, without architecture that expressed the desire for symmetry prevalent at the time. It was thought desirable to change this, and to carry out this task Moltke chose to involve the Court Builder Nicolai Eigtved, who had been made responsible for the new town plan and thus for Amalienborg. Nicolai (or Niels) Eigtved had travelled widely around Europe in the 1720s and 30s, when what was known as the rococo style spread from France to the rest of the continent, and through his work the new light style came to feature in a number of buildings in Copenhagen and north Zealand. Eigtved and Moltke had also already cooperated on several building projects, so the Lord Chamberlain knew that Eigtved was capable of creating a magnificent monument to the absolute monarch.

The main features of the town plan

Eigtved's influence came to be of fundamental importance to Frederiksstaden. While Amalienborg, in all that matters, is his work, he also drew up the town plan for the whole new area and set out the guidelines for the other construction work, and all the facades of the town houses had to be approved by him before they were built. His

Amalienborg seen from the Copenhagen Opera House. The flag on Christian VIII's Palace tells us that either Prince Joachim or Princess Benedikte acted as regent on this day.

Amaliegade looking towards the Citadel (Kastellet). A typical feature of Frederiksstaden is the co-ordinated line of windows and cornices, even though the houses vary considerably in style.

town plan rapidly became reality, with the two axes, the lengthwise axis (Amaliegade) between Toldboden and Sankt Annæ Plads crossing a transverse axis (Frederiksgade) running between the harbour and the planned church, which in Lord Chamberlain Moltke's thinking was conceived on a grand scale. The King wanted a church included in the town plan, and thanks to his aunt, Princess Charlotte Amalie, he could make available a square plot on the other side of Bredgade which was ideally suited to the purpose. The transverse axis found a natural location running from the church-site to the harbour, and in the course of just a few weeks Eigtved drew up plans for the octagonal "square" with an equestrian statue in the centre, surrounded by four identical rococo mansions, which elegantly combined Saxon and French style features. Seen as a whole it was a solution that took inspiration from Paris, where in 1748 there had been a major architectural competition about the design of the octagonal square that is now known as Place de la Concorde. The draft designs submitted for the competition were known to Eigtved, and provided the most important direct inspiration for Amalienborg.

Eigtved's original overall plans for Frederiksstaden have been lost, and there are some uncertainties as to what decisions were taken when, but evidently the town plan was under constant revision during the first few years. It is uncertain, for instance, at what stage the area's five other great mansions were included in the plans. One of them forms the corner of Amaliegade and Sankt Annæ Plads, and the four others, which face onto Bredgade, take up most of the stretch of that street from Sankt Annæ Plads to Fredericiagade. The mansion which is today known as Odd Fellow Palace was built for Minister and Count C.A. von Berckentin, and apart from the Amalienborg palaces it is the most spectacular building in Frederiksstaden. It was completed in 1755 and is placed, in Parisian style, to be viewed as the concluding point of Dronningens Tværgade; like Amalienborg it is designed in a light rococo style. This is not accidental, since Eigtved probably contributed as architect in the construction of all the palaces and probably also had decisive influence on their location. Similarly, it was Eigtved's idea to establish a garden at Kastellet to provide a visual focus at the end of Amaliegade.

Odd Fellow Palace at the end of Dronningens Tværgade. Built for C.A. von Berckentin in cooperation with Nicolai Eigtved.

The equestrian statue of Christian X (1870-1947), from 1954, on the edge of St Annæ Square (Sankt Annæ Plads), by sculptor Einar Utzon-Frank. This monument to the King, who rode through Copenhagen each morning from his residence in Amalienborg, is the latest artistic addition to Frederiksstaden.

From an early stage there were also ideas of including a hospital in the plan. After the accession of Frederik V to the throne Lord Chamberlain Moltke had worked on a plan for the incoming government in which he stressed the importance of creating better conditions for science, art, and – in the same sentence – care of the poor and the sick, while he also laid out some guidelines for his view of an ideal society: piety should be prevalent, and the King's laws and orders should not be seen as oppression but as support for enterprising inhabitants. Frederiksstaden as a whole can be seen as having been planned on the basis of Moltke's ideas of what the state should be. The town district links together God (the church), the

King (the equestrian statue), the nobility (the mansions) and the surrounding enterprising bourgeoisie, with Frederiks Hospital, which today houses a museum – Designmuseum Danmark – completing the picture. Although it cannot be determined whether the hospital was included in the earliest plans, it fits into the symbolism of Frederiksstaden; on the hospital's foundation stone from 1752 it is mentioned that it will accommodate 300 patients, i.e. the number of years celebrated at the Jubilee for Frederik V's royal dynasty.

It is clear, however, that the actual Amalienborg axis was certainly in place before the Jubilee was celebrated at the end of October 1749. Eigtved had the plans ready for Amalienborg and Frederik's Church and had defined the general guidelines for all the other buildings. The Jubilee became a grand celebration of royal power, with the town decorated to the point of being unrecognizable, and extraordinary efforts were made to renovate the normally malodorous streets of Copenhagen. The festivities culminated on the third day, when the King to great jubilation laid the foundation stone of the new church which was to be named after him, and that was the starting signal for the construction of the new district of town.

Building Frederiksstaden

With the specific exception of the church, Frederiksstaden was completed in the 25 years that followed the Jubilee. Building began in 1750, and the first "houses for the bourgeoisie", which all had to be 17 metres wide and 82 metres deep, with windows and cornices at the same level, were completed in the following year. It was not possible to find people to take on construction to fill the whole area, because despite the favourable economic conditions at the time there were not a sufficient number of well-to-do citizens, but a large part of the area was built on in the course of the 1750s. All of Frederiksstaden's nine great mansions were built within the first decade, as was Frederik's Hospital, which was completed in 1757. Since in the mid-1760s there were still large unused areas in the neighbourhood of Kastellet, another hospital, known as Almindelig Hospital (the General Hospital) was built immediately adjacent to the first hospital and facing Toldbodgade. It was not intended for care of the sick, like Frederiks Hospital, however, but rather had the nature of a workhouse or an institution for care of the needy.

From among the many buildings, gardens and details in Frederiksstaden only the most important, from the district's central axes, have been selected to be described here in greater detail: Amalienborg, the equestrian statue, and Frederik's Church.

Frederik's Hospital was built during the years 1752-57 in accordance with drawings by Nicolai Eigtved and Lauritz de Thurah. The hospital was closed in 1910. After major refurbishment the Designmuseum Danmark was able to welcome visitors to the old hospital from 1926 onwards.

Amalienborg

While most of the sites were allocated by the Copenhagen town authorities, the King had reserved the right to choose those who would own and build the Amalienborg mansions, and it was naturally a great privilege to be awarded one of the four sites. The best situated of them, as regards angles of light and ground conditions, was the southern plot closest to Bredgade, which was reserved in advance by Moltke himself. Although the facades of the four palaces were to follow Eigtved's drawings meticulously, there was a large measure of freedom allowed to the owner-builders in matters of interior organization and decoration, and in addition they had freedom of choice as to how the area behind each mansion was laid out and arranged as gardens and service-buildings. Moltke's palace became the most distinguished of the four, in a class of its own, both with regard to the layout of the grounds and the interior decoration. It was unique among the palaces in that the interior was also designed by Nicolai Eigtved, and it is now the most elegant preserved rococo interior in Denmark. When Eigtved died in 1754 the interior was completed by the French architect Nicolas-Henri Jardin, who created the neoclassical banquet-room in 1757, which is also considered to be a masterpiece in its category.

In 1750 Moltke offered the task of building what is now Christian IX's Palace to the young Baron and Councillor Severin Leopoldus Løvenskiold, but after a few years he had to abandon completing the building because of a lack of financial resources. He succeeded in transferring the project to the widowed Countess Anna Sophie Schack in 1754, however, and the first occupant of the palace was her grandson, Count Hans Schack, who moved in during 1757, when he married Moltke's daughter. Moltke himself helped with the completion of the palace by putting his own craftsmen to work on it.

The building that is now Frederik VIII's Palace was erected for Joachim Brockdorff, who was a baron, Privy Councillor, honorary member of the Danish Royal Academy of Sciences and Letters and Knight of the Order of the Elephant. He did not manage to enjoy the palace for long, however, since it was not finished until 1760 and both he and his wife died in 1763. The palace was then first transferred to Moltke, but was subsequently bought by Frederik V in 1766 and thus became the first of the four palaces to come into royal possession.

The last of the four palaces, now Christian VIII's Palace, was constructed by Christian Frederik Levetzau, who was a Count, Privy Councillor, Lieutenant General of the Infantry and Knight of the Order of the Elephant. He never lived in the palace, however, and on his death in 1756 it was left to his widow.

Nicolai Eigtved died in 1754 and so did not see his masterpiece completed. The supervision of the project was loyally continued by his competitor, Laurits de Thurah, who had previously left the town in a rage when his own proposal for Frederiksstaden was rejected in the planning stages. When he died in 1759 the leading role was taken over by Nicolas-Henri Jardin, who did not, however, have significant influence on the finished result.

The equestrian statue

The equestrian statue of Frederik V turned out to be the most costly monument in Denmark's history, but also one of the finest. On Eigtved's very first sketches there was a statue marked in the centre of the open area between the four mansions, and the rid-

The erection of the equestrian statue on 16 August 1768 was a major event in Copenhagen with cannon salutes and military music. The royal family watched from the balcony of Moltke's Palace. One notes that the artist has included the dome of Frederik's Church, which was in fact far from finished. Work on the dome was stopped by J.F. Struensee a few years later. There are two very similar drawings of this event, but the artist cannot be identified with certainty.

The equestrian statue with Frederik V in profile. From the standard flying over Frederik VIII's Palace one can see that members of the family of the Crown Prince are at home.

er could of course be none other than the King himself. There were no Danish artists who could be entrusted with the task of creating the statue, however; it would have been a daunting prospect. The monument had to be the very heart of a structure that was virtually an architectural illustration of the theory of the state under the absolute monarchy: the King is positioned in front of God's house, from which he receives the power and strength to deliver peace and well-being to the people, with the nobility as the connecting link, represented by the four palaces. It was also challenging that the statue had to be adapted to a pre-chosen site and not vice versa, as had been the case, for instance, in the creation of Louis XV's square (Place de la Concorde) in Paris. The choice fell on a young talented Frenchman named Jacques François-Joseph Saly, who was brought to Copenhagen in 1753. The choice of Saly was daring, in that he had not previously made an equestrian statue, but he was highly recommended and was also given favourable working conditions for the project. The terms of his appointment included making him Professor at the Academy of Fine Arts in 1754 and he became Director there after Eigtved's death; the responsibilities attached to this post were in large part the reason that his work on the statue took more than double the time originally planned.

Saly prepared a wax model which was approved in 1755; this established the scale of the work, and from the outset it was clear that the style was to be modern neoclassical, but the question of how the King should be portrayed required lengthy consideration. On the one hand it was necessary to provide a portrait-style likeness, but since the object of the work was to glorify the concept of the absolute monarchy, Saly chose to present Frederik V sitting in state on his horse like a Roman emperor, with armour and laurel wreath. Naturally there had to be innumerable sketches and models before a satisfactory result was achieved, and the practical challenges were also immense, so it was not until 1768 that the statue could finally be cast in bronze. The work was nevertheless far from finished at that point, because the base was also to be a work of art in its own right. Then the supply of money began to dry up, however, since the statue was a burden on the resources of the Danish Asiatic Company, which had agreed, in 1754, to finance the project. Many of the shareholders were angry at the company's president, who had arranged the donation – and who was in fact A.G. Moltke. Saly therefore had to make a more modest version of the base than had been planned, providing it with four tablets describing the King's achievements as a protector of art, science, industry and trade. When the base was ready and the square had been cobbled it was at last possible to unveil the statue, in 1771. There was still a railing missing around the monument, however, and that was not finished until 1774, when the foundry in Frederiksværk pro-

vided it as a gift to the King. Shortly before then Saly had gone back to France because he felt that he had been cheated of an agreed fee.

The budget for the statue was originally 35,000 rigsdaler. This was an unrealistically low estimate for a commission of this type, but the actual price rose to an extreme level. The costs in the end ran up to over half a million rigsdaler, which was far more than it cost to build all the rest of Amalienborg. Nevertheless, one could – and still can – take pleasure in the fact that it became one of Europe's finest monuments of its kind.

Frederik's Church (the Marble Church)

When Frederik V laid the foundation stone for his church at the ceremony on 30 October 1749, there was doubtless no one present who could have imagined what the building would come to cost in terms of both money and patience. Although the church was the most grandly ambitious element in Frederiksstaden, it was to be all of 145 years before a complete church stood on the site – and the finished product was rather more modest than the originally planned version.

A handful of drawings by Eigtved are known from the beginning of the 1750s, and they retain the same light decorative rococo style as the Amalienborg palaces. Rococo was already beginning to slip out of fashion while the palaces were being built, however, and the church-building committee therefore began to collect alternative proposals from both local and French architects. Most of the projects had the same ground-plan as Eigtved's version: a round, central church area with a large drum-borne cupola flanked by two small bell-towers. In the twenty years during which work was actively done on the case no fewer than 16 proposals and partial schemes succeeded each other, and at least six architects were involved. The most important drawings came from Nicholas-Henri Jardin, who had been brought to Denmark after Eigtved's death, as already mentioned. His drawings were in the new neoclassical style that succeeded rococo, and building work began on the basis of those plans in 1756. It had been decided, however, that the church should be built in Norwegian marble, and this turned out to be unrealistically costly. A fatal blow was dealt to the building project when Frederik V died in 1766. The King's death meant that Moltke lost influence, and suddenly there was an absence of motivation to promote the construction work and secure financing for it. In the first instance the budget was halved, but in 1770 Christian VII was persuaded, on the advice of Struensee, to stop construction of the church, and this also brought to a halt the construction of the planned build-

Nicolai Eigtved's second proposal for Frederik's Church, which was presented in March 1752. One can easily see the stylistic similarity with Amalienborg, and the lowermost levels correspond completely to the facades of the four palaces.

ings around it. Jardin's marble church had by that time reached a height of some nine metres above ground.

The church then remained a ruin for a century. The precious marble was later to some extent reused, but much of it was stolen from the building site. Although many attempts were made to restart construction, there was insufficient willingness to finance a church that would come anywhere near matching the level of ambition from the founding of Frederiksstaden. It was not until after the financier C.F. Tietgen had bought the site, in 1874, that planning was taken up seriously again. Tietgen at first employed the architect Christian Zwingmann for the purpose, but he became ill and transferred the project to another prominent architect of the time, Ferdinand Meldahl, who drew up plans for a smaller church, in a form of Roman baroque, which could be built on top of the original still-standing walls. The plans involved abandoning the side-towers and building a significantly lower rotunda. Instead of Norwegian marble it was limestone that was used for building, although this did not prevent the name "the Marble Church" continuing to be used. Construction of the present church was begun in 1877 and completed in 1894.

The completion of Frederik's Church meant the achievement of an aesthetically coherent way of concluding the overall composition of Frederiksstaden. Even though the church was smaller than had originally been planned, it placed Frederik V in the intended connection with the Almighty and created a transverse axis that corresponded to Eigtved's original concept. The Amalienborg axis has moreover in recent decades received two conspicuous additions on the harbour side in the form of the waterfront garden called Amaliehaven, and the Opera House, aligned with it on the other side of the water. Both were funded by A.P. Møller og Hustru Chastine Mc-Kinney Møllers Fond til almene Formaal. (See photos on page 14 and back cover.)

Royalty at Amalienborg

Christian VII (1766-1808)
As already mentioned, the fire at Christiansborg in 1794 destroyed the palace only half a century after it had been completed. Although the lives of the members of the Royal Family were saved, the loss of the palace was a national catastrophe. It was the grandest and most valuable palace in Northern Europe, and it burned down to the ground in the course of one night, with almost all of its splendid fur-

nishings and enormous quantities of invaluable works of art. This of course left the Royal Family in a difficult practical situation, but it turned out that a solution could quite readily be found. A.G. Moltke had died one and a half years earlier, and the Foreign Minister, A.P. Bernstorff, had been selected to be executor of his estate. It therefore took only a simple transaction to arrange for Christian VII to purchase Moltke's Palace and thus acquire an acceptable royal residence for himself. But it was also possible to solve the housing problem of Crown Prince Frederik (VI); a few days later Schack's Palace was also bought. It was considerably less expensive, but it was in poor condition, since it had been let out for twenty years. It therefore required thorough renovation before it could serve as a residence for

The ruins of the Marble Church painted before 1857 by Hans Ditlev Christian Martens. For decades the ruined church was a popular and atmospheric excursion spot for the citizens of the city.

the Crown Prince and Crown Princess, and so initially they also had to live in Moltke's Palace. This was a convenient arrangement for the organization of matters of state, since it was the Crown Prince who in fact bore the authority to rule on behalf of his insane father.

Eventually the King's half-brother bought Levetzau's Palace, on the other side of Frederiksgade, in which Nicolai Abildgaard created a neoclassical interior – still well-preserved today – for the bel étage. This meant that the whole of Amalienborg was then in royal ownership, since the King already owned Brockdorff's Palace, which had been bought by Frederik V in 1766. That mansion, however, was in no way suitable to be a royal residence, because it had been converted for use as a college for officers in 1767. One could hardly claim that this was a fitting use of such fine premises, but in fact the building functioned as a training academy until 1826, at first for the army and then for the navy. The ground floor of the palace was arranged as living quarters for the officers, and the first floor contained teaching rooms; the ceiling in the Great Hall – which was used as a fencing area – was lowered to make room for dormitories on the mezzanine level. There was therefore not much left of the original Brockdorff's Palace. The distinguishing clock on the facade was added so that the Life Guards on duty outside could keep to the schedule of sentry shifts.

When the Royal Family moved in, this gave rise to a rather major alteration to the architecture of Amalienborg. In the first place an extra storey was added between the palaces and the adjacent corner pavilions situated towards Amaliegade and Frederiksgade. Originally there was only a connecting ground floor building, as one can still detect from the facades. The alterations gave the exterior of Amalienborg a more solid appearance, but contributed to alleviating the space problems that confronted the Royal Family and their large household staff.

Secondly, the architect for the alterations, C.F. Harsdorff, was allowed to construct the Colonnade, which is the pillared structure that connects the two southernmost palaces. The purpose of the Colonnade was simply to make it possible to go from one palace to the other without using a carriage, because Crown Prince Frederik (VI), as the functioning Head of State, had to be in frequent contact with his father, the mentally ill king. Although only a few metres separated the palaces it was not appropriate for royalty to go out into the street, and so a closed walkway was built above the Ionic pillars of the Colonnade.

The Royal Family's period of residence at Amalienborg was considered at that time to be a temporary solution, and because it was generally expected that Christiansborg would imminently be rebuilt, the Colonnade was constructed out of wood, plastered so that it looked like stone. Despite this low-cost method of construction the Colonnade turned out to fit in so well with its surroundings that it was allowed to remain standing even when it lost its original purpose after Christian VII's death in 1808, and it is still in use today.

In the period of over 200 years in which Amalienborg has served as a royal residence there has been a tradition that the reigning monarch has lived in one palace while the heir to the throne has lived in another, and that is still current practice today. It is a ma-

The Colonnade and the equestrian statue seen from the southern part of Amaliegade. Graphic print by J. Borchert, c. 1900, belonging to the Amalienborg Museum.

Amalienborg and Frederiksstaden

jor advantage of the construction – and a unique one in an international context – that the generations can divide up the palaces between themselves, and this is probably also part of the reason that Amalienborg has become the permanent royal residence. There follows a chronological summary of how the Royal House has made use of the different palaces over the years.

Frederik VI (1808-1839)

Since Frederik VI had had Schack's Palace renovated while he was Crown Prince, his accession to the throne did not give rise to major changes in his own living quarters. In the same year he bought the mansion in Amaliegade later known as the "Yellow Palace" (its facade was coated with traditional yellow lime-wash in 1842, and it has retained that appearance since). Throughout much of his life Frederik VI was to divide his time between Schack's Palace (now Christian IX's Palace) and a house in nearby Toldbodgade in which he installed his mistress, Bente Rafsted, who was later known as Fru Dannemand, in 1808.

The fact that Amalienborg became the permanent residence of the Royal House was in part the result of Frederik VI's unfortunate political manoeuvring during the Napoleonic wars. In 1800 the architect C.F. Hansen had received approval of his plans for the rebuilding of Christiansborg as a royal residence, but the economic circumstances could not support rapid reconstruction. The bombardment of Copenhagen in 1807, the State bankruptcy in 1813 and the loss of Norway in 1814 did not add up to a context conducive to ambitious palace-building, and although by 1828 the construction work had progressed to the point when the Royal Family could have moved in, this was no longer seen as desirable. They had settled in Amalienborg, and neither Frederik VI nor Prince Christian (VIII) wished to move. After Frederik VI's death in 1839 the Dowager Queen Marie continued to live in Schack's Palace until her death in 1852.

The most noteworthy change at Amalienborg in Frederik VI's time was the renovation of Brockdorff's Palace. The Officer Training College moved out of the exceedingly worn-down palace in 1826 when Prince Frederik (VII) became engaged to Frederik VI's daughter Vilhelmine. A thorough rebuilding operation was put in hand, and the architect Jørgen Hansen Koch achieved the creation of a neoclassical homogeneity in the palace.

Christian VIII (1839-1848)

With Christian VIII's accession to the throne in 1839 Levetzau's Palace (now Christian VIII's Palace) for the first time became the residence of a reigning monarch. In the same year he moved his brother-in-law, Vilhelm of Hesse-Kassel, who was Commandant of Copenhagen, into Brockdorff's Palace (now Frederik VIII's Palace); he remained there until his death in 1867. Christian VIII died in 1848, but the Dowager Queen Caroline Amalie lived in Amalienborg until her death in 1881. Like her husband she was interested in intellectual pursuits, and her library is still to be found on the bel étage of the palace. The furnishings are made of carved wood in neo-Gothic style and the bookshelves are full of nineteenth-century literature in a variety of languages.

The Yellow Palace in Amaliegade, designed by N.-H. Jardin and built in 1759-64. Today the palace houses the administration offices of the Royal Court.

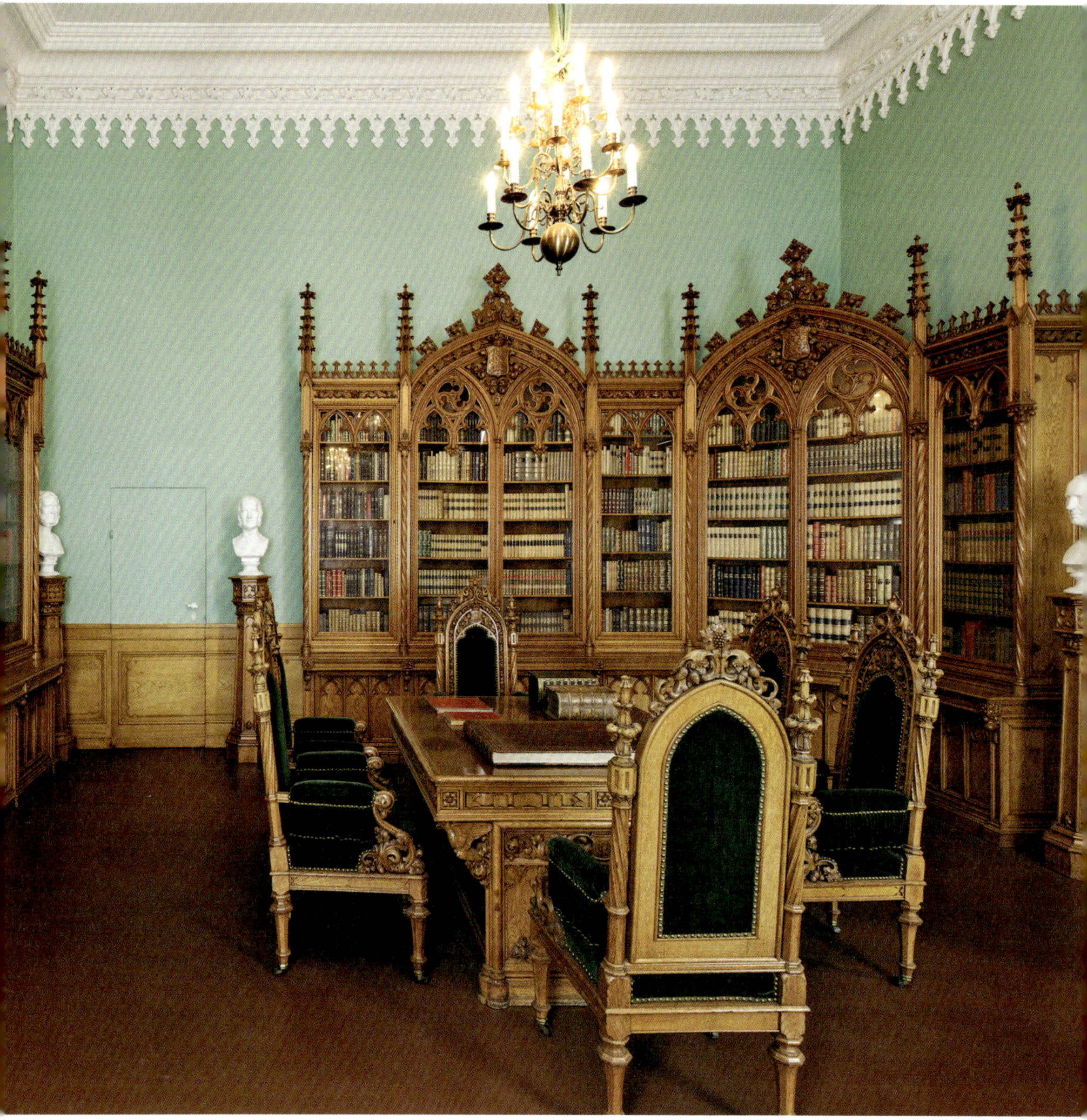

After Christian VIII's death Levetzau's Palace was renamed after him, but one can still see the coat of arms of the original owner on the palace; the Levetzau family stipulated that it should remain there when the palace was taken over by the Royal House in 1794.

Frederik VII (1848-1863)

The marriage of Prince Frederik (VII) and Frederik VI's daughter Vilhemine only lasted until 1834, by which time the King had had enough of his son-in-law's dissolute lifestyle. Frederik VI forced through a divorce, and Prince Frederik was sent into exile in Fredericia, in Jutland, where he remained until King Frederik VI's death in 1839.

Although he had lived in Brockdorff's Palace as a young man, Frederik VII was the only monarch since Frederik V who did not live in Amalienborg during the period of his reign. This was partly because his marriage to Countess Danner aroused so much animosity among the aristocracy and the upper bourgeoisie that Copenhagen became an unpleasant place for him to be. The couple eventually settled in in the castle at Jægerspris, some 50 km from Copenhagen, which they bought from the state in 1854.

Frederik VII was the last of the absolute monarchs. He renounced absolute power on 22 March 1848, only a couple of months after his accession, and a few years later, as an innovative measure, constitutionally-based institutions were moved into Amalienborg. Thus parts of Moltke's Palace (now Christian VII's Palace) were taken over by the Foreign Ministry and used by it from 1852 until 1885, and during the period 1855-1864 both the Supreme Court and the Foreign Ministry occupied parts of Schack's Palace (now Christian IX's Palace). The Foreign Ministry's last period of time in Amalienborg was in Levetzau's Palace (now Christian VIII's Palace) from 1885 to 1898, when Prince Christian (X) and Princess Alexandrine took it over. With the end of the absolute monarchy the royal palaces were transferred to state ownership, and since then the state has placed a number of them at the disposal of the Royal House.

Christian IX (1863-1906)

The Oldenburg line of the royal dynasty, in whose honour Frederiksstaden was built, died out with Frederik VII. This made way for the new Glücksburg line, with Christian IX, who was already a familiar figure at Amalienborg. After the death of Christian's father, Duke Vilhelm of Schleswig-Holstein-Sonderburg-Glücksburg, in 1831, Frederik

The Gothic Library was furnished for Dowager Queen Caroline Amalie in 1852. The architect was Christian V. Nielsen; the cabinetmaker P.L. Wolff and the woodcarver H.V. Brinkopff made the furniture. The library is considered the only consistently executed neo-Gothic room in Denmark. The Dowager Queen received many of the 19th century's prominent cultural personalities here, and busts of several of them were placed in the library. The shelves contain mostly nineteenth-century literature.

The view of the palace square from Frederik VIII's study, which is furnished in the Renaissance Revival style and can be seen as part of the Royal Danish Collection at Amalienborg.

VI and Queen Marie had taken the 13-year-old Prince Christian into their home, since they themselves had no sons, and he had therefore spent many years of his youth in Schack's Palace. When he became king it was also in Schack's Palace that he and Queen Louise took up residence after having lived in the "Yellow Palace" since their marriage in 1842. Schack's Palace remained the royal couple's official residence until they died, in 1898 and 1906 respectively, and after that the palace was officially named after Christian IX.

When the rebuilt Christiansborg burned down in 1884, Moltke's splendid palace, now Christian VII's Palace, was given its present functions: providing representation areas and guest apartments, as a consequence of the loss of the royal representation apartments in Christiansborg.

Frederik VIII (1906-1912)

After Christian IX's death, the new king, Frederik VIII, and his siblings decided that Christian IX's Palace should be allowed to remain untouched as a place where they could all gather and keep their parents' memory alive. Christian IX's Palace therefore remained mainly unlived-in until 1967, although the Dowager Empress of Russia, the former Princess Dagmar, stayed there for a short time after she had escaped from Russia during the 1917 revolution.

Following spread: The Great Hall of Christian VII's Palace is considered one of Europe's finest rococo rooms. This palace, which was then known as Moltke's Palace, was the only one of the four palaces whose interior was designed by Nicolai Eigtved, who created the most splendid interior of his career in this hall.

Frederik VIII and Queen Lovisa had moved into Brockdorff's Palace (now Frederik VIII's Palace) in 1869, when they were married, and the accession to the throne therefore did not give rise to any changes, for them or for the new Crown Prince and Crown Princess, who had moved into Christian VIII's Palace (previously Levetzau's) in 1899. After his death Frederik VIII was honoured, like his father, by having his palace renamed after him, so that then all four palaces had names of kings. The Dowager Queen Lovisa lived in the palace until her death in 1926.

Christian X (1912-1947)

Christian X and Queen Alexandrine lived in Christian VIII's Palace from the end of 1899 until they died, in 1947 and 1952 respectively. They were the first royal couple who did not reside at Amalienborg only temporarily but officially stated that this was the seat of the monarchy. This happened in the context of the Parliamentary Crisis of 1920, but the development had been prepared a few years earlier in connection with the completion of the third – and present – version of Christiansborg. Living quarters had in fact been provided in the new palace for the royal couple, but

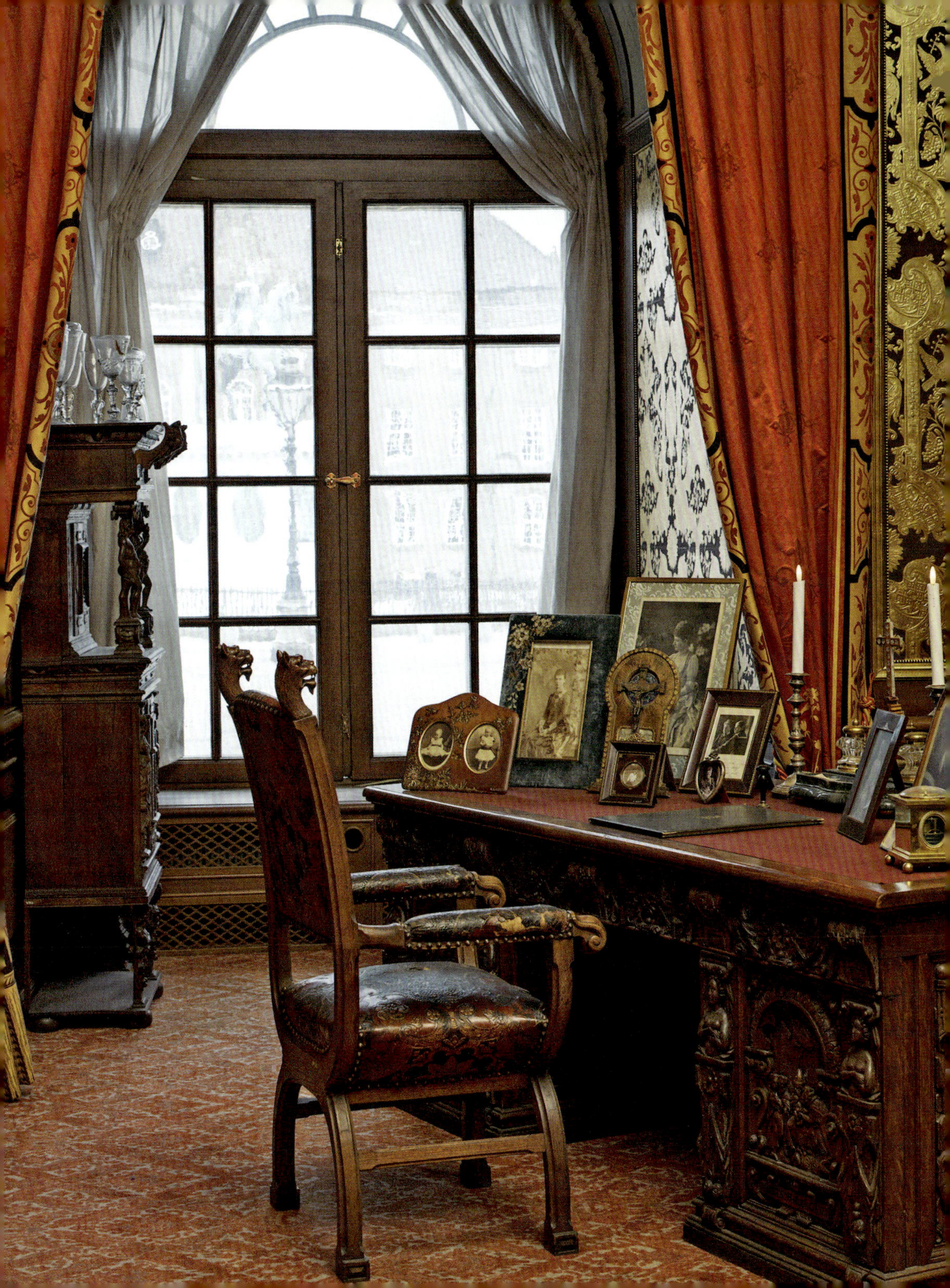

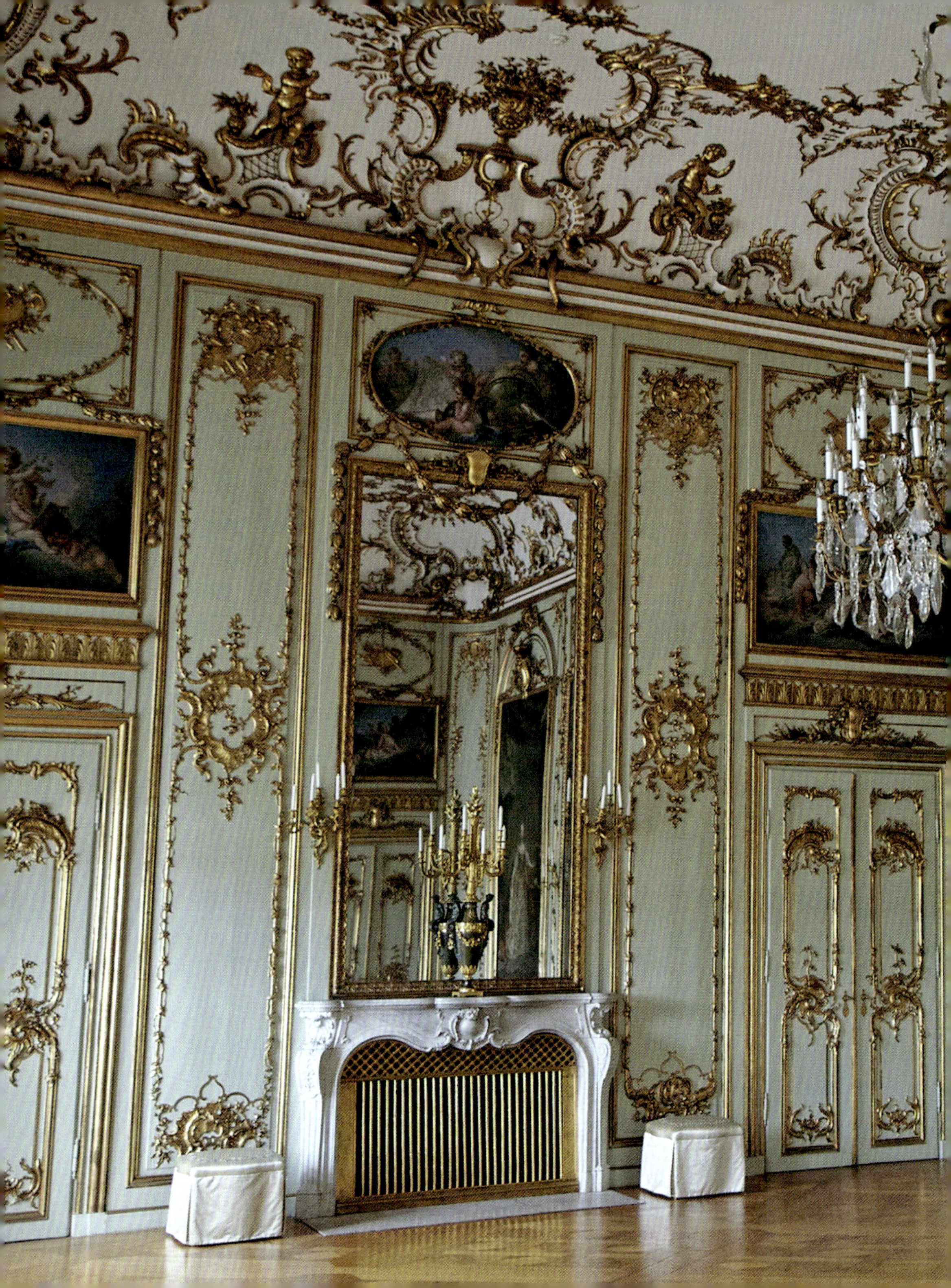

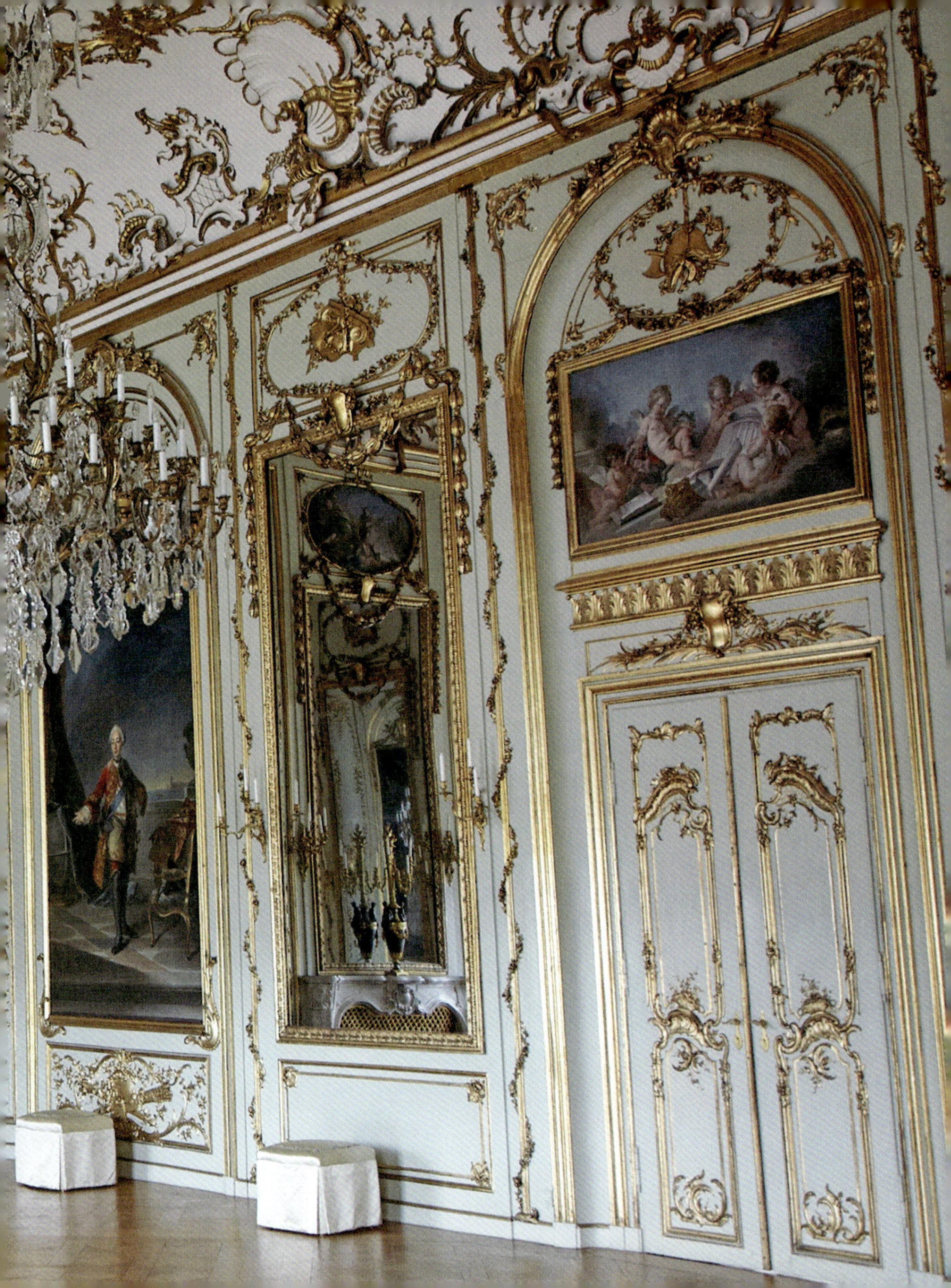

exactly as Frederik VI had done back in 1828, Christian X and Queen Alexandrine chose to decline graciously and to continue to live in Amalienborg.

Christian X was the first king at Amalienborg to experience seeing the square full of people with a political purpose. This happened in 1915 with the Women's Campaign (it was a celebration of the newly won right to vote), and then with the 1920 Parliamentary Crisis (when there was a demonstration against the King's arbitrary dismissal of the Government), and later, in 1933, with the Farmers' Campaign (calling for better conditions for agriculture). Another dramatic point in Amalienborg's history occurred in the form of the skirmish on 19 September 1944, which left lasting traces in the shape of bullet holes in the walls.

Frederik IX (1947-1972)

Frederik VIII's Palace, the former Naval Officer Academy, also, appropriately enough, became the residence of the "Sailor King", Frederik IX, and thus also

Queen Alexandrine (Christian X's Queen) in the Garden Room in Christian VIII's Palace, c. 1940.

Damage to Amalienborg from German gunfire on 19 September 1944 is physically preserved as part of the history of the residence today. The Life Guards were disarmed in 1943, so the Royal House was protected by what were known as the Police Guards. When the occupation forces decided to arrest the Guards from Amalienborg along with the rest of the Danish police force they did not do so without meeting resistance. Two policemen and the palace administrator were wounded, while no fewer than twenty German soldiers were killed and several others wounded. The memorial tablet below the holes was erected in 1952.

Amalienborg and Frederiksstaden 51

Amalienborg and Frederiksstaden

the childhood home of Denmark's present Queen and her sisters. Crown Prince Frederik and Crown Princess Ingrid moved into the palace after their wedding in 1935.

Queen Ingrid made a distinct impression on Amalienborg, in particular on Frederik VIII's Palace; she was very interested in interior design and had a talent for it which she has passed on to her daughter, Her Majesty the Queen. Among other things Queen Ingrid made the interior decoration of Amalienborg more colourful than it had been previously, and the royal couple also brought modern furniture design into the old palaces. After Frederik IX's death in 1972 Queen Ingrid lived in the palace until her death in 2000.

Amalienborg today

In the course of more than two hundred years as a royal residence Amalienborg has naturally undergone many changes. The many occupants, with the movements of taste that fluctuate over time, have made their mark on the palaces, and the present members of the Royal House have also left their mark on the buildings in noteworthy fashion. It is well-known that Her Majesty the Queen is closely engaged with Amalienborg's development and has been deeply involved in the various renovations that have taken place. This is particularly true of Christian IX's Palace, where the Queen and Prince Consort have their residence, but Christian VII's Palace has also benefitted from contributions by the Queen. During the thorough restoration of Moltke's old palace that was undertaken between 1982 and 1996, the Queen took an active part in decisions about the interior restoration, and this is reflected, for instance, in the choice of colours – a matter in which the Queen cannot be accused of having an over-cautious nature. The renovation work was carried out with great respect for Eigtved's and N.-H. Jardin's interiors, which are still well-preserved, since the palace has not had permanent residents since the death of Christian VII.

Their Royal Highnesses Crown Prince Frederik and Crown Princess Mary have also put a personal stamp on Amalienborg. After Queen Ingrid's death, in the years 2004-2010 Frederik VIII's Palace underwent complete renovation and its interior was totally redesigned. The Crown Prince and Crown Princess chose in this context to introduce modern art into Amalienborg. On their initiative the interior of the palace has been adorned by works of art by a number of Danish artists of our time, and the palace as a whole has become an ambitious example of a modern royal residence, in which new and old are combined. This is of

Frederik IX's study, which was transferred from Frederik VIII's Palace to Christian VIII's and is now part of the Amalienborg Museum's permanent display.

course not the first time that contemporary artists have made their mark on Amalienborg – Nicolai Abildgaard's interiors from 1794 were after all fashionable in their own time – but it is part of the charm of the place that it continues to be able to accommodate new initiatives within the pre-existing context.

It can be expected that future generations of the Royal House will also take possession of Amalienborg's palaces in new ways, and that Frederik V will continue to sit triumphantly on his horse as the constant centre-point of his ideal town district.

When one visits Amalienborg Palace Square (Amalienborg Slotplads), it is well worth looking down. The pretty mosaic by Johan Daniel Herholdt was laid in 1886 and restored in the 1990s.

A corner of the courtyard behind Christian VIII's Palace. Each palace at Amalienborg has an area behind it with a courtyard, garden, and outbuildings which for example house offices for staff of the Royal Household.

Following spread: The changing of the guards at Amalienborg attracts an audience year round. The Life Guards were created by Frederik III in 1658 as an infantry regiment in the Danish army with the particular mission of protecting the country's highest authority, that is, the king. Originally, the Life Guards wore red uniforms, and yet today the soldiers wear red on festive occasions. For everyday use the soldiers wear the dark-blue jacket that was introduced during the 19th century, when the uniforms more or less got their current appearance, with bearskin hats and stripes on their trousers.

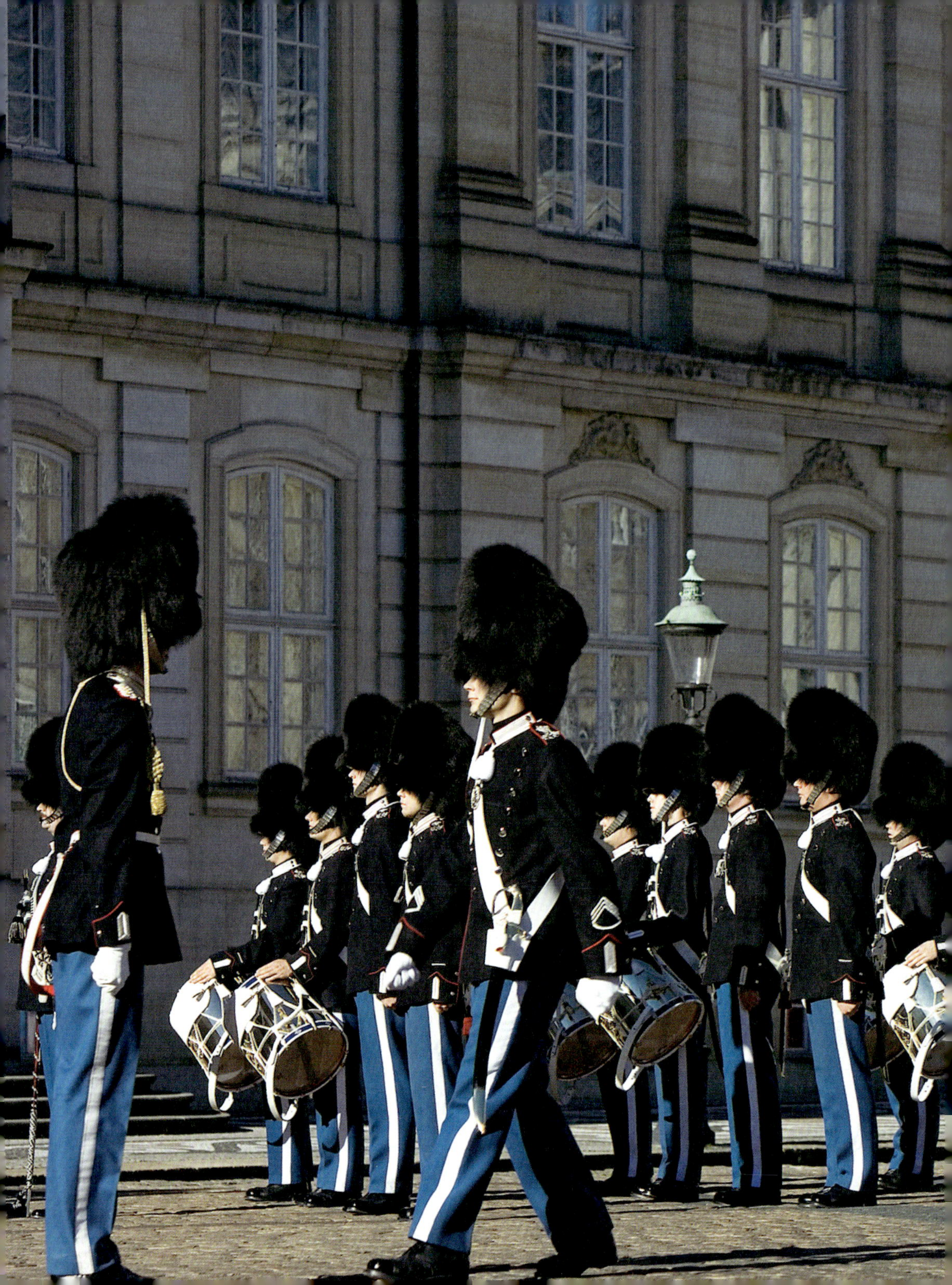

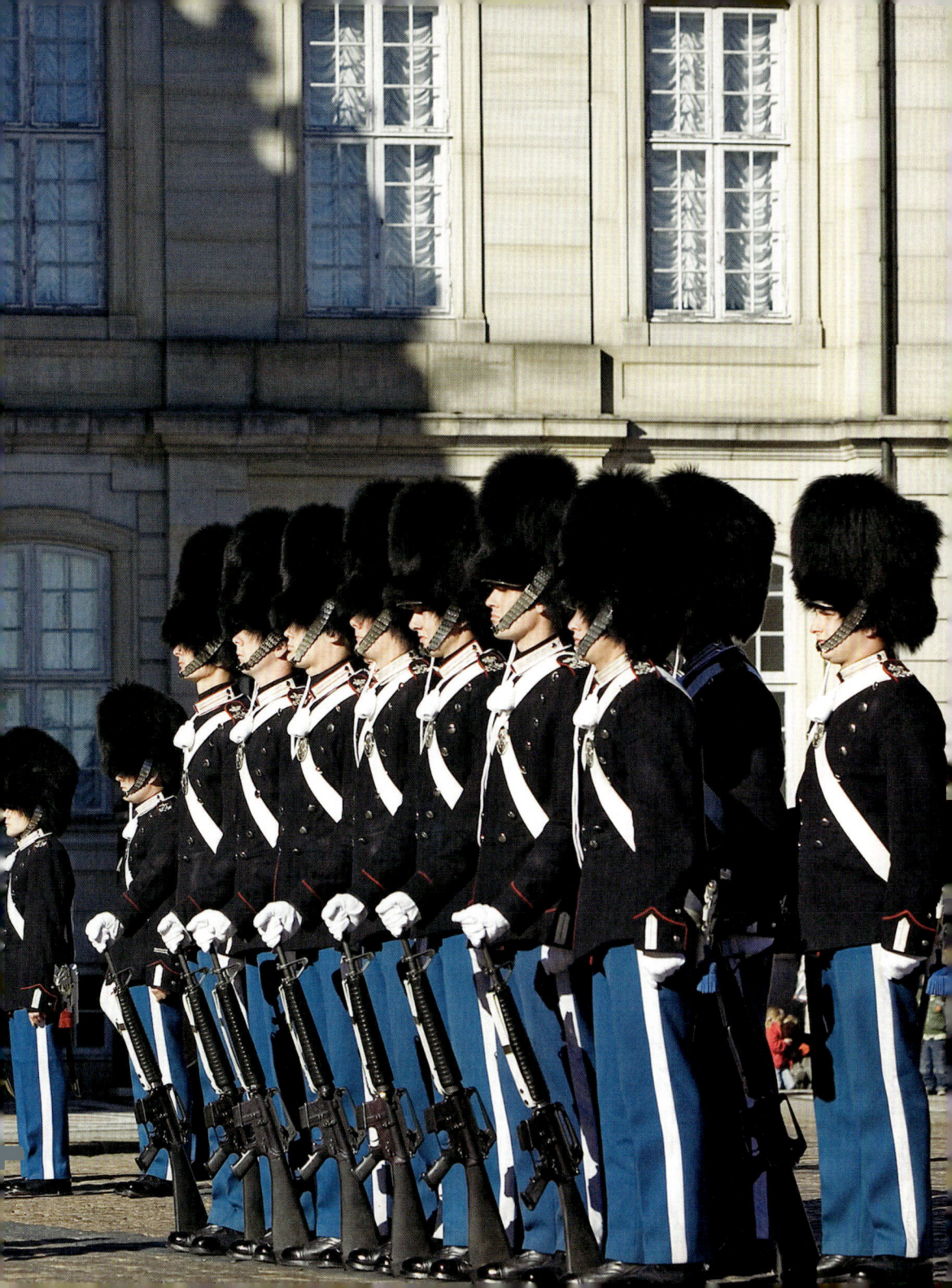

BIBLIOGRAPHY AND FURTHER READING

Bertelsen, Jens et al. (eds.): *Frederik VIII's Palace: Restoration, Rebuilding, Artistic Decoration,* Slots- og Ejendomsstyrelsen 2010.
– A wide-ranging and in-depth account of the restoration of Frederik VIII's Palace 2004-2010. Also available in Danish.

Christiansen, Jørgen Hegner (ed.): *Architectura 21,* Selskabet for Arkitekturhistorie 1999. Published as an off-print with the title *Gud – Konge – By:* Frederiksstaden 250 år (vol. 2) on the occasion of an exhibition about Frederiksstaden held by the Danish Museum of Art & Design in 1999.
– Separate articles about the history of major elements in Frederiksstaden: the town plan, the palaces, the town houses, the church, the equestrian statue, the hospitals and the gardens, together with an article about A.G. Moltke. In Danish with English summaries.

Larsen, Jørgen, Thomas Larsen and Bjarke Ørsted: *Amalienborg,* Gyldendal 2010.
– A wide-ranging book in large format which provides a unique insight into life at Amalienborg and many of the different features that ensure that the residences are smoothly run. The book contains extensive interviews with the Queen and Prince Consort and many illustrations from present-day Amalienborg. In Danish.

Rasmussen, Kjeld (ed.): *Amalienborg: De kongelige palæer, gemakker og haver,* Borgen 1999.
– A compact and accessible presentation of Amalienborg's history, describing the individual palaces and providing pictures of all the most important rooms. In Danish.

VISIT AMALIENBORG

Amalienborg is one of Denmark's most popular visitor attractions. Many people come to see the fine buildings and the Changing of the Guard – and to be photographed together with a Guard. There are also various opportunities to see some of the interiors.

The Amalienborg Museum in Christian VIII's Palace is open all year round apart from a few closing days. Visitors have an opportunity to visit the Glücksburg kings' studies, which are part of the permanent exhibit on the ground floor, and experience the beautiful bel étage, which features interiors by Nicolai Abildgaard.

The Agency for Palaces and Cultural Properties also arranges guided tours of Christian VII's Palace when it is not being used by the royal family.

www.kongernessamling.dk

Amalienborg and Frederiksstaden
The Palace and the Royal Quarter

Copyright © 2015
The Royal Danish Collection and Historika / Gads Forlag A/S

ISBN: 978-87-93229-10-5
First edition, first print run

Printed in Lithuania

Text: Jens Gunni Busck
Edited by Birgit Jenvold
Translated from Danish by Joan F. Davidson
Cover and graphic design Lene Nørgaard, Propel
Printed by Clemenstrykkeriet, Lithuania

Illustrations:
p. 6: Berit Møller, p. 15, 18-19, 41, 44, 47, 50, 52: Kongernes Samling,
p. 7, 12, 16, 24-25, 26, 28, 43, 48-49: Christopher Sand-Iversen,
p. 2, 21, 32-33: Det Kongelige Bibliotek, p. 4, 8-9, 10-11, 22, 27, 30, 35, 51, 54, 55: Kasper Monty, p. 36: Danmarks Kunstbibliotek,
p. 39: Det Nationalhistoriske Museum (foto: Kit Weiss),
p. 56-57: Jens Astrup, Scanpix

Photocopying may only be undertaken at institutions that have concluded agreements with COPY-Dan and may only be undertaken within the limitations established by the agreement in question.

CO₂ neutrale tryksager
KLIMANEUTRALISERET
Cert.nr. 0017/DK

MIX
Paper from responsible sources
FSC® C122712